PRAY-4-
BREAKTHROUGH

PRAY-4-BREAKTHROUGH

How to Speak God's Word
over Your Marriage
in under 5 Minutes

BY

Nykia Coleman

XULON PRESS

Xulon Press Elite
2301 Lucien Way #415, Maitland, FL 32751
407.339.4217 / www.xulonpress.com

© 2023 by NYKIA COLEMAN

All rights reserved solely by the author. The author guarantees all contents are original and do not infringe upon the legal rights of any other person or work. No part of this book may be reproduced in any form without the permission of the author. The views expressed in this book are not necessarily those of the publisher.

Due to the changing nature of the Internet, if there are any web addresses, links, or URLs included in this manuscript, these may have been altered and may no longer be accessible. The views and opinions shared in this book belong solely to the author and do not necessarily reflect those of the publisher. The publisher, therefore, disclaims responsibility for the views or opinions expressed within the work.

Unless otherwise indicated, Scripture quotations taken from the Good News Translation (GNT). Copyright © 1992 American Bible Society. Used by permission. All rights reserved. Scripture quotations taken from the Amplified Bible (AMP). Copyright © 1954, 1958, 1962, 1964, 1965, 1987 by The Lockman Foundation. Used by permission. All rights reserved. Scripture quotations taken from the New King James Version (NKJV). Copyright © 1982 by Thomas Nelson, Inc. Used by permission. All rights reserved. Scripture quotations taken from the Holy Bible, New International Version (NIV). Copyright © 1973, 1978, 1984, 2011 by Biblica, Inc.™. Used by permission. All rights reserved. Scripture quotations taken from the Holy Bible, New Living Translation (NLT). Copyright ©1996, 2004, 2007 by Tyndale House Foundation. Used by permission of Tyndale House Publishers, Inc. Scripture quotations taken from The Holy Bible, Berean Study Bible (BSB). Copyright ©2016, 2018 by Bible Hub. Used by Permission. All Rights Reserved Worldwide.

Paperback ISBN-13: 978-1-66286-866-5
Ebook ISBN-13: 978-1-66286-867-2

Dedication

This book is dedicated to my husband, Avery M. Coleman. I admire you for the man you are becoming in Christ, and I value your personal commitment to doing life with me. May our three beautiful children, Avery, Samuel, and Zylah, inherit a legacy of faith and respect for the marriage covenant.

Acknowledgments

I give thanks to my Lord and Savior.
In addition, I am grateful to my paternal Grandparents, J.T. and Earline Burnside,, who demonstrated that real love never fails. Love never gives up, never losses faith, is always hopeful, and endures through every circumstance (*1 Corinthians 13:7, New Living Translation*).

A special thanks to my mother, Carol E. Sapp, who taught me it is better to love than not to love at all.

Finally, I am grateful for my spiritual family: Senior Pastors Gary and Anne Martin, Pastors Corey and Amber White, Pastors Zachary and

Nykia Coleman

Ashley Martin, Pastors Nicholas and Jessica Smith, Pastors Aaron and Adrienne Crane, Pastors Jeremy and Krista Sharp, Bishop Matthew and Archie Bride, Pastors Robert and Patricia "Diahann" Johnson, Chris and Ivy Jones, Wylie and Equalla Foster, Richard and Jan Lauletta, Dana and Tammie Stevenson, Lauree Goodwin, Andre and Taji Burnside, Edie Burnside, Dan and Maureen Arthur, Scott and Erika Laing, Kevin and Mandy Themm, Darrell and Wendy Johnson, Brian and Keiana Bridgeforth, Harrison and Mary MaKau, Aaron and Rosie Belton, Felix and Nancy Chege-Mwania, Linda Sherbon, Linda DiNeiri, Luckita Massey, Janice Ross, Jonathan and Skye Padilla, and all subscribers to the Pray4Breakthrough ministration.

Introduction

Over the past couple of years, I have witnessed a strong attack against marriages. This book was birthed out of the overflow of the Holy Spirit as I prayed and interceded for numerous marriages. I asked God to lead me in how to pray for the marriages that were broken, fractured, and in need of healing. This prayer book addresses some of the common causes of marital separation, and is designed to help marital couples fight for their marriage and avoid the divisiveness of divorce.

Key Scriptures

I will not break my covenant with him or take back even one promise I made him.

Psalm 89:34 (Good News Translation)

Therefore, what God has united and joined together, man must not separate [by divorce].

Mark 10:9 (Amplified Bible)

Thou shalt also decree a thing, and it shall be established unto thee: and the light shall shine upon thy ways.

Job 22:28 (King James Bible)

As the rain and the snow come down from heaven and do not return to it without watering the earth and making it bud and flourish, so that it yields seed for the sower and bread for the eater, so is my word that goes out from my mouth: It will not return to me empty, but will accomplish what I desire and achieve the purpose for which I sent it.

Isaiah 55:10-11 (New International Version)

God is not a man, so he does not lie. He is not human, so he does not change his mind. Has he ever spoken and failed to act? Has he ever promised and not carried it through?

Numbers 23:19 (New Living Translation)

For no matter how many promises God has made, they are "Yes" in Christ. And so through him the "Amen" is spoken by us to the glory of God.

2 Corinthians 1:20 (New International Version)

So David and his troops went up to Baal-perazim and defeated the Philistines there. "God did it!" David exclaimed. "He used me to burst through my enemies like a raging flood!" So they named that place Baal-perazim (which means "the Lord who bursts through").

1 Chronicles 14:11 (New Living Translation)

Now Jesus was telling the disciples a parable to make the point that all times they ought to pray and not give up and lose heart.

Luke 18:1 (Amplified Bible)

And they have defeated him by the blood of the Lamb and by their testimony. And they did not love their lives so much that they were afraid to die.

Revelation 12:11 (New Living Translation)

Therefore, I tell you, whatever you ask for in prayer, believe that you have received it, and it will be yours.

>   *Mark 11:24 (New International Version)*

And I will do whatever you ask in my name, so that the Father may be glorified in the Son.

>   *John 14:13 (New International Version)*

Table Of Contents

Dedication vii
Acknowledgements ix
Introduction. xi
Key Scriptures xiii
Day 1 1
Day 2 3
Day 3 6
Day 4 8
Day 5 10
Day 6 12
Day 7 14
Day 8 16
Day 9 18
Day 10 20
Day 11 22

Day 12 24
Day 13 26
Day 14 28
Day 15 30
Day 16 32
Day 17 34
Day 18 36
Day 19 39
Day 20 41
Day 21 44
Day 22 46
Day 23 48
Day 24 50
Day 25 52
Day 26 54
Day 27 56
Day 28 59
Day 29 61
Day 30 63
Day 31 65
Day 32 67
Day 33 69
Day 34 71

Day 35 73
Day 36 75
Day 37 77
Day 38 79
Day 39 81
Day 40 83
Day 41 85
Day 42 87
Day 43 89
Day 44 91
Day 45 93
Day 46 95
Day 47 97
Day 48 99
Day 49 101
Day 50 103
Day 51 105
Day 52 108
Day 53 110
Day 54 112
Day 55 114
Day 56 116
Day 57 118

Day 58 120
Day 59 122
Day 60 124
Married Couples and Years Together.... 127

Day 1

"Should you not fear me?" declares the Lord. "Should you not tremble in my presence? I made the sand a boundary for the sea, an everlasting barrier it cannot cross. The waves may roll, but they cannot prevail; they may roar, but they cannot cross it."

Jeremiah 5:22
(New International Version)

Prayer

Heavenly Father, I revere You as the all-powerful, mighty Creator; the awesome God who created all things. I thank You for Your magnificent handiwork. I thank You that Your strength, authority, and voice still have control over even the fiercest winds and the wildest storms. Every boundary line You have set must be obeyed by everything in the world, including everything above and below the surface.

Right now, I receive supernatural protection for our marriage. I pronounce God's peace over every source of tension, strife, and conflict. I declare our marriage untouchable by all satanic, wicked, and demonic forces.

Endow my spouse and me with a spirit of wisdom to establish biblical standards and boundaries for our marriage that is consistent with Your holy Word.

I form a boundary line with the shed blood of Jesus, an everlasting barrier to preserve and protect our marriage against all seducing, enticing, divisive, and homewrecking spirts. I concur with God's Word, and declare our marriage to be holy, blessed, and wonderful. Amen!

Day 2

When I saw their fear, I stood and said to the nobles and officials, and the rest of the people: "Do not be afraid of them; [confidently] remember the Lord who is great and awesome, and [with courage from Him] fight for your brothers, your sons, your daughters, your wives, and for your homes."

Nehemiah 4:14
(Amplified Bible)

Prayer

Father in heaven, You are my confidence; the One whom I place all my trust. Even when it seems like I am surrounded by giants greater than me, You have promised in Your Word that those who put their trust in God shall not be disappointed. I, therefore, resolve in my heart to have complete faith and full assurance in Your promises.

Grant my spouse and me the fortitude and perseverance to weather every storm, challenge, and adversity. I decree I shall not cast away my confidence for in it is great reward. I confess my spouse, as well as our home, are my top priorities.

Right now, I break agreement with every timid and passive spirit. I declare I shall walk in the confidence and boldness of Christ, to fight, defend, guard, protect, and bless our marriage. Today, I make the sensible choice to break ties with any person who does not respect our marriage covenant.

I repent for the moments I gave into a spirit of compromise, allowing people who did not have pure intentions to speak into our marriage. Lord, forgive me for the times I wanted to give up and lose heart. In Jesus' name, I pray for divine empowerment and strength to honor my commitment to our marriage.

Help my spouse and I to live out Your agape love to contribute to the harmony and well-being of our marriage today and always. Amen!

Day 3

"The latter glory of this house will be greater than the former," says the LORD of hosts, "and in this place, I shall give [the ultimate] peace and prosperity," declares the LORD of hosts.

Haggai 2:9
(Amplified Bible)

Prayer

Jesus, You are the Prince of Peace, whom I worship. You are the One who created peace and promotes it. I am grateful for Your clearly expressed desires to bless my home and marriage.

May my spouse and I remain agents of Your peace when interacting and communicating with one another. Now, I speak to every storm and say, "Peace, be still by the matchless power of God Almighty." I prophesy that every disturbance is suddenly becoming calm.

Lord, I invite the splendor and radiance of Your Holy Spirit into our marriage and home. May a peaceful cloud cover our home from the ceilings to the floor, and from the front yard curb to the backyard. May Your spirit of peace rest upon every person who enters or exits our home.

In Jesus' name, I bind every spirit of hostility, anger, malice, rage, and lack of self-control, and I render those spirits ineffectual. In Jesus' name, I cancel all of their evil works and agendas through the blood of Jesus Christ and through the accomplished work of the cross. I decree rivers of Your glory and peace shall flood our marriage uncontested.

God display Your power and restore the full measure of Your peace, safety, welfare, happiness, health, and prosperity in our marriage in Jesus' name. Amen!

Day 4

> *This man's name was Nabal, and his wife, Abigail, was a sensible and beautiful woman. But Nabal, a descendant of Caleb, was crude and mean in all his dealings.*
>
> *1 Samuel 25:3*
> *(New Living Translation)*

Prayer

Heavenly Father, I recognize You as love. You are the One who lovingly lifts all my heavy burdens. You are the epitome of what a loving spouse, companion, and entrusted friend should look like. God, You embody all that love should represent, reflect, and portray.

Lord, I bring every offense my spouse or I have committed to Your altar. I curse the spirit of any trauma from past hurts, offenses, infidelity, broken promises, betrayals, insults, and slander. Under the authority of Jesus Christ, I strip and take away the power of every abusive spirit: whether emotional, physical, psychological, verbal, or sexual.

I speak God's healing to all hardness and calcifications of the heart in Jesus' name, and I release God's solace, comfort, peace, forgiveness, and restoration over our marriage. For these things, I pray and praise You heavenly Father. Amen!

Day 5

> *Give honor to marriage, and remain faithful to one another in marriage. God will surely judge people who are immoral and those who commit adultery.*
>
> *Hebrews 13:4*
> *(New Living Translation)*

Prayer

Heavenly Father, I worship You as a holy God. You are perfect, upright, and just in all respects. I thank You for the sanctity You have placed around the institution of marriage. All people are accountable to the Word of God whether the person believes in God or not.

In Jesus' name, I break all ungodly soul ties, yokes, entanglements, and alliances my spouse or I have formed outside our marriage intentionally or unintentionally. I sprinkle the blood of Jesus upon ourselves and upon our marriage bed cleansing it of all contaminations, defilements, and impurities. I pull down every stronghold, unholy desire, ungodly imagination, and unclean fantasy, and I take it captive and make it obedient to Jesus Christ. I use the keys of the kingdom and I bind the spirit of divorce, and I release a renewed commitment to covenant.

In Jesus' name, I activate the power of *Galatians 3:13*, and I break every ancestral and generational curse of divorce and marital separation that exists in our family lineage.

I release a renewed responsibility and devotion to God-the Father, God-the Son, and God-the Holy Spirit upon my spouse and me through the blood covenant of Jesus Christ. Amen!

Day 6

You have heard that it was said, 'you shall not commit adultery.' But I tell you that anyone who looks at a woman lustfully has already committed adultery with her in his heart.

Matthew 5:27-28
(New International Version)

Prayer

Heavenly Father, I thank You for holiness, godliness, and righteousness. I thank You for the godly expectation and standard You have established for marriage. May this biblical truth resonate in my heart and in the heart of my spouse today and always.

In Jesus' name, I bind spirits of carnality, lust, adultery, perversion, and sexual addiction of any kind that would attempt to infiltrate our marriage, and I lay them at the footstool of Jesus. I release a spirit of holiness upon us.

Anoint both our eyes and grant us spiritual discernment to abstain from the lust of the flesh. Empower my spouse and me to walk in godly wisdom at all times and live a self-controlled life.

In Jesus' name, I extinguish the spirt of Jezebel, and every foul and unclean spirit with the shed blood of Jesus, and I cancel all their evil works to destroy our marriage.

I speak God's peace, healing, and restoration to every dry, barren, and fruitless part of our marriage in the wonderful name of Jesus. Amen!

Day 7

Wisdom will save you also from the adulterous woman, from the wayward woman with her seductive words, who has left the partner of her youth and ignored the covenant she made before God. Surely her house leads down to death and her paths to the spirits of the dead. None who go to her return or attain the path of life.

Proverbs 2:16-19
(New International Version)

Prayer

Heavenly Father, I thank You that You are a covenant keeper. You have exalted Your name and Your Word above everything.

Bestow upon my spouse and me a spirit of wisdom to flee, depart, and blatantly reject the advances of any adulterous person in Jesus' name. Grant my spouse and me spiritual discernment to recognize that all seducing advances, propositions, and compliments only pave a way toward demise: demise of finances, respect, health, honor, and right standing with God.

In Jesus' name, I revoke the authority and power of all flirtatious and seductive spirits, and I cancel all of their missions to sow discord into the life of our marriage.

Lord, You alone, possess the power to change the heart of man. So, I, ask for You to direct our eyes and heart, back to You first, before we refocus our attention back to each other as it should be.

Lord, I give You praise for Your abundant grace and mercy, and Your heart to heal all that is broken in our marriage in Jesus' name. Amen!

Day 8

Then they prayed, "Lord, you know everyone's heart. Show us which of these two you have chosen to take over this apostolic ministry, which Judas left to go where he belongs." Then they cast lots, and the lot fell to Matthias; so he was added to the eleven apostles.

Acts 1:24-26
(New International Version)

Prayer

Heavenly Father, I'm thankful that You understand the human heart. There is nothing hidden from You, and no one can deceive You.

Today, I ask that You examine the heart of my spouse and me. Replace any spirit of dishonesty with a spirit of truthfulness, and displace a spirit of carnality with a spirit of holiness. Create in my spouse and me a clean heart and renovate every dark place with the light of God.

I speak a divine encounter and total conversion of our hearts after the order of Saul on the Damascus Road. We shall become the people You have envisioned for us before the foundations of the world were laid. In Jesus' name, turn all the bad in our hearts to good, so we can be completely devoted to Christ, and to each other from now on.

I prophetically speak by faith that all who behold us shall marvel at the transformative work You accomplish in our marriage and through us for the glory of Your holy name. Amen!

Day 9

Don't copy the behavior and customs of this world, but let God transform you into a new person by changing the way you think. Then you will learn to know God's will for you, which is good and pleasing and perfect.

Romans 12:2
(New Living Translation)

Prayer

Heavenly Father You are perfection. What my spouse and I have seen You say and do, grant us the strength to put it into practice.

Right now, I lay prostrate before Your altar, and I cover the mind, will, emotions, and thoughts of my spouse and me with the shed blood of

Jesus. I capture every thought that exalts itself against God's Word, and I bring it into the complete compliance of Jesus Christ.

Give us a heart of love, forgiveness, compassion, sincerity, and understanding. Transform us into new people who reflects God's character, nature, and reputation. Pour out Your Holy Spirit so powerfully that we become a different person according to *1 Samuel 10:6*.

Right now, I come against spirits of bad habits, questionable motives and intentions, and all ungodly ambitions, and I release the fire of God against them in Jesus' name. I invoke the conviction of the Holy Spirit upon us both.

Endow my spouse and me with a supernatural ability to resist the works of darkness, temptations, worldliness, and unrighteousness. Each day, allow us to become more and more Christ-centered which is good, pleasing, and perfects our marriage in Jesus' glorious name. Amen!

Day 10

Do not lie to each other, since you have taken off your old self with its practices and have put on the new self, which is being renewed in knowledge in the image of its Creator.

Colossians 3:9-10
(New International Version)

Prayer

Dear heavenly Father, You are the God of all creation, and I thank You for my spouse's existence.

Grant my spouse and me a compassionate heart to see each other through the eyes of grace. Let us put on robes of humility, mutual courtesy, and kindness.

Today, I come against spirits of intolerance, lack of patience, judgmentalism, and criticism. In Jesus' name, I resist every lying, deceptive, and treacherous spirit and I strip them of their power and influence. Cause my spouse and me to decrease so that You may increase in us.

Lord, I, ask that You remain the focal point and foundation of our marriage. Permit us to increase in wisdom, knowledge, and understanding so we can know how to serve You better and love each other from a sincere and pure heart.

May we both come to know our heavenly purpose for which You created us. Reveal to us Your divine plan as to why You brought us together so we can cooperate and further Your kingdom's agenda.

Let Your kingdom come and let Your holy will be done in the life of our marriage, this day and forever in Jesus' name. Amen!

Day 11

> *"I, the LORD, search the minds and test the hearts of people. I treat each of them according to the way they live, according to what they do."*
>
> Jeremiah 17:10
> (Good News Translation)

Prayer

Heavenly Father, I appreciate You as a just and righteous Judge. You are God who probes the mind and examines and inspects the heart. You care more about a man's heart than his external appearance, public applause, job titles, luxury vehicles, income, collegiate degrees, and academic credentials.

I entrust my spouse and me into the palms of Your hands, and I ask that You evaluate our hearts. Reveal and expose those areas where my spouse and me are alienated from You. Bring us to a place of true repentance and reconciliation before You regarding the things we have said and did wrong.

In Jesus' name, I bind every counterfeit and false humility spirit, and I release the fruit of the Spirit upon my spouse and me according to *Galatians 5:22-23*. Let us wear a bullet-proof vest of love, joy, peace, forbearance, kindness, goodness, faithfulness, gentleness, and self-control.

Arrest our attention and remind us that one of the fundamental goals of our marriage is to emulate how Christ loved the church in Jesus' name I pray. Amen!

Day 12

But the LORD said to him, "Pay no attention to how tall and handsome he is. I have rejected him because I do not judge as people judge. They look at the outward appearance, but I look at the heart."
1 Samuel 16:7
(Good News Translation)

Prayer

God, I thank You that You examine the motives of each individual. People's charisma and good looks are never enough to deceive You.

Today, I pray the motives of my spouse and me are in alignment with Your perfect and holy will. I take authority over all evil thoughts and desires and bring them into the submission of Jesus

Christ. I combat every spirit of error and deception, and I stop all of their evil works, deeds, and maneuvers in their tracks in Jesus' name.

Lord, I ask that You whistle at us from every direction and captivate our attention. Give us ears to hear Your voice and to never follow the voice of a stranger according to *John 10:5*. I decree the enemy shall no longer be able to control our minds or infect the core of our hearts to impact our marriage in a negative way.

Almighty God, cleanse all our thoughts and motives because only the spiritually receptive can perceive the thoughts, plans, and purposes of God in Jesus' name. Amen!

Day 13

So, He said to them, "You are the ones who declare yourselves just and upright in the sight of men, but God knows your hearts [your thoughts, your desires, your secrets]; for that which is highly esteemed among men is detestable in the sight of God."

Luke 16:15
(Amplified Bible)

Prayer

Heavenly Father, I praise You for Your microscopic view of man's heart. You know every detail of our criminal, deviant, rebellious, and immoral history. There is nothing about our human nature that can be hidden from You. You know our shame, guilt, greed, and every infectious and corrupt thing about the heart.

Lord, I ask that You seize my heart and the heart of my spouse in such a huge way that it disturbs hell and causes heaven to celebrate in Jesus' name. Make us into people who truly care what You think and respect Your authority. *John 15:5* confirms apart from You we can do nothing.

In Jesus' name, I bind spirits of pride, greed, and double mindedness and command them to be consumed by the fire of the Holy Ghost. I release righteousness, integrity, and the Spirit of Truth upon my spouse and me. I declare we shall no longer be divided between two opinions.

I speak God's renewal, favor, unity, and blessings over our marriage now in Jesus' name. Amen!

Day 14

The wise woman builds her house [on a foundation of godly precepts, and her household thrives], but the foolish one [who lacks spiritual insight] tears it down with her own hands [by ignoring godly principles].

Proverbs 14:1
(Amplified Bible)

Prayer

Heavenly Father, I adore You. I revere Your great, wonderful, and excellent name.

Today, I make a personal commitment to build our house on Your godly commandments, laws, and statues so that our marriage and home can thrive, prosper, grow, and become everything good You envisioned for it.

When we are tempted to curse, let us bless. When we are tempted to yell, empower us with self-restraint. When we are anxious and frustrated, let us find rest and peace in Your presence. When we're tempted to be vindictive, let us put down our sword. Help us to resist going our own way and yielding to a carnal understanding.

Proverbs 24:3 says, it is by wisdom a house is built and by understanding it is established. So, release a spirit of wisdom upon my spouse and me. Put God's words in our mouths to produce life and a good harvest for our marriage and home.

As a prophetic act each day I awake, I decree I am a spouse who builds my house and doesn't tear it down.

I proclaim God's blessings of peace, healing, restoration, and love over our marriage and home today and always, in Jesus' name. Amen!

Day 15

Then the elders and all the people at the gate said, "We are witnesses. May the LORD make the woman who is coming into your home like Rachel and Leah, who together built up the family of Israel. May you have standing in Ephrathah and be famous in Bethlehem."

Ruth 4:11
(New International Version)

Prayer

Heavenly Father, I praise You because You are a constant encourager. You delight to edify and build up Your people.

I invoke the Lord's blessings upon our marriage and declare our family shall be built up after the order of Rachel and Leah. I decree we shall benefit and bless one another in Jesus' name.

Right now, I'm seizing the opportunity to detach myself from every destructive spirit. I renounce and break agreement with any spirit that would cause me to violate my marital covenant between my spouse, God, and me in Jesus' name.

Malachi 2:16 confirms God hates divorce. So, Lord, I sincerely ask for You to give my spouse and me Your heart. Instill in us a hatred for the things You hate, and a love for the things You value and cherish.

You are a God who delights in love, peace, faithfulness, and unity. Empower my spouse and me to embrace these qualities so our marriage can be bonded in faith, complete unity, forgiveness, and unconditional love.

Merciful Father, beautify and bless our marriage this day and always in Jesus' name. Amen!

Day 16

Who may ascend the mountain of the LORD? Who may stand in his holy place? The one who has clean hands and a pure heart, who does not trust in an idol or swear by a false god.

Psalms 24:3-4
(New International Version)

Prayer

Heavenly Father, You are a bondage breaker.

Lord, I, ask that You correct any iniquities in the heart of my spouse and me that contribute to the breakdown of our marriage. By Your grace and mercy, keep us from becoming ensnared or entangled with any yoke of bondage again.

Psalm 32:7 states You surround us with songs of deliverance. I lay claim to that deliverance and petition the court of heaven for it to come quickly and eradicate every hidden and concealed sin. In Jesus' name, I ask for supernatural deliverance from lying, cheating, pride, jealousy, gambling, deceitfulness, idolatry, false religions, and all forms of abuse and addictions.

Right now, I rebuke and cast out all spirits of discord, disunity, and disharmony, and I command these spirits to never return in the powerful name of Jesus. Wash my spouse and me in Your redemptive blood and help us to walk in integrity, honesty, and pureness of heart.

I speak by faith that my spouse and me shall be righteous in thought, deed, and motives; fit to draw near to God in this life and in heaven also in Jesus' name. Amen!

Day 17

Through pride and presumption come nothing but strife, but [skillful and godly] wisdom is with those who welcome [well-advised] counsel.

Proverbs 13:10
(Amplified Bible)

Prayer

Heavenly Father, You are the great I AM.

Proverbs 3:34 states You give grace to the humble. I bow down in genuine humility before You, and I place my spouse and me in Your hands.

In Jesus' name, I cast aside spirits of pridefulness, stubbornness, vanity, and haughtiness. I release upon my spouse and me humility and reverence for God. We submit to Your authority and allow You to have complete jurisdiction in all areas of our marriage.

Increase our spiritual appetite for more of Your presence. Lord, set Your blazing and consuming fire against all works of the flesh and unrighteousness. Strategically place my spouse and me around true God-fearing men and women who speak the truth about God's word regarding the covenant of marriage in Jesus' name.

Release Your archangel, Michael, to uproot and overthrow anyone whose motives are evil toward our marriage, in Jesus' name.

Pour out an enormous release of Your heavenly blessings of prosperity, hope, and peace upon our marriage this day and for the rest of our lives together, in Jesus' name. Amen!

Day 18

"Woe to me!" I cried. "I am ruined! For I am a man of unclean lips, and I live among a people of unclean lips, and my eyes have seen the King, the LORD Almighty." Then one of the seraphim flew to me with a live coal in his hand which he had taken with tongs from the altar. With it he touched my mouth and said, "See this has touched your lips; your guilt is taken away and your sin is atoned for."
Isaiah 6:5-7
(New International Version)

Prayer

Heavenly Father, I thank You for forgiveness of sins. You blot out all iniquities and remember them no more. Thank You for the mercy of not seeing my spouse and me through the stain of our countless sins, but rather through a massive mirror of grace.

Lord, release an angel to come down and touch our mouths with the tongs of Your altar burning out every source of corrupt speech, perverse words, and unacceptable conversation. Avert our attention away from all communication that is dishonorable and displeasing in Your sight. Cause my spouse and me to appreciate the grace that covers and atones for our sins through the shed blood of Jesus Christ.

Without delay, I usurp Christ's authority, and I permanently cut every ungodly communication line that offends the Lord. I decree all communication channels, including, but not limited to, verbal, nonverbal, written, auditory, visual, and all forms of social media are irrevocably shattered, through the authority of God's Word and the power of the Holy Spirit.

Nykia Coleman

Lord, may my spouse and me become so God-conscious that we will choose not to sin against You with our words in Jesus' name. Amen!

Day 19

Run away from sexual immorality [in any form, whether thought or behavior, whether visual or written]. Every other sin that a man commits is outside the body, but the one who is sexually immoral sins against his own body.

1 Corinthians 6:18
(Amplified Bible)

Prayer

Heavenly Father, You are the author of life. I acknowledge my body is the temple of the Holy Spirit, and I am to glorify You in my body and spirit.

Today, I employ the keys of the kingdom and I bind all seducing, alluring, and enticing spirits that would pull and tug my spouse away from our marriage. In Jesus' name, I break all ungodly soul ties formed in the past or present, and cut off any attempt of unhealthy soul ties forming in the future. Wherever the enemy has my spouse or me blinded to the hazardous effects of sexual immorality, I pray You expose the lie and replace it with the truth of Your Holy Word.

May we present our bodies to God as a living sacrifice, holy and pleasing to Him, which is our reasonable act of worship. Grant my spouse and me the power to reject all lewdness, promiscuity, masturbation, fornication, adultery, and all forms of sexual immorality.

For the glory of God, grant us the courage, capacity, and competence to flee from every unclean thought, deed, or action, whether visual or written.

I speak God's fidelity and sacredness over our marriage forever in Jesus' name. Amen!

Day 20

For this is the will of God, that you be sanctified [separated and set apart from sin]: that you abstain and back away from sexual immorality; that each of you know how to control his own body in holiness and honor [being available for God's purpose and separated from things profane], not [to be used] in lustful passion, like the Gentiles who do not know God and are ignorant of His will.

1 Thessalonians 4:3-5
(Amplified Bible)

Prayer

You are the Lord of Hosts, heavenly Father. I thank You for clarifying Your vision, purpose, and intention for marriage. *Proverbs 30:5* confirms every Word of God is flawless. The Word of God contains no error, and it proves true. God's word is superior to all other forms of knowledge, opinions, ideas, and conjectures.

Lord, I ask, for You to construct and erect a thorn bush hedge of protection around our marriage in accordance with *Hosea 2:6-7*. Set us apart from everything profane and perverse that would pollute our bodies in Jesus' name.

I oppose all of the enemy's strategies and schemes with the Word of God, the blood of Jesus, and the power of the Holy Spirit. I speak a spontaneous abortion to all of the enemy's plans orchestrated against our marriage, and declare God's will to prevail.

May a tsunami of God's love flood our marital foundation. I prophesy there shall be a meteoric rise in our mutual attraction, and my spouse and me shall find each other irresistible.

I speak God's richest blessings upon our marriage, and I prophesy it shall resemble the image and landscape of a beautiful paradise beyond human imagination in Jesus' name. Amen!

Day 21

The mouth of an immoral woman is a deep pit [deep and inescapable]; He who is cursed by the LORD [because of his adulterous sin] will fall into it.

Proverbs 22:14
(Amplified Bible)

Prayer

Heavenly Father, I praise You because You are my rear guard. You protect me from the front, back, and on all sides. Grant me a discerning spirit, and let no man deceive me according to *Matthew 24:4*.

I ask for angelic reinforcement to put to death every spirit of adultery once and for all. Release Your warring angels immediately in accordance with *2 Kings 19:35*, and completely annihilate the enemy's camp. Let not one of my adversaries remain standing in Jesus' name. Lord, protect my spouse and me from every immoral man and woman. By Your mercy, let us not fall prey to the wicked pit of adultery.

In Jesus' name, I revoke all self-imposed curses spoken over our marriage from our own lips as a result of our own anger, frustration, jealousy, and disappointment. By the power of Jesus' name, I break every ancestral covenant and oath of death, divorce, and marital separation operating in our family tree.

In Jesus' name, I command my spouse to be released from every demonic stronghold, ungodly soul tie, bondage, entanglement, and attraction formed with anyone other than me. I prophesy today a shift is on the horizon, and the evil work of every adulterous spirit is coming to a complete end.

I speak God's blessings of healing and restoration to every broken place. Amen!

Day 22

Now the LORD God said, "It is not good (beneficial) for the man to be alone; I will make him a helper [one who balances him-a counterpart who is] suitable and complimentary to him."

Genesis 2:18
(Amplified Bible)

Prayer

Heavenly Father, I'm thankful You recognize the importance of companionship. It is not Your will for me to be alone. *Isaiah 49:16* states You have inscribed my name in Your palms and my walls are continually before You. I choose to believe that our marriage is also eternally recorded in Your memory. I believe You have determined our marriage valuable, important, and worth defending.

In Jesus' name, I cast down every lie of the enemy that suggests and implies I am insignificant to my spouse and our marriage. I come against spirits of deception, lies, nonacceptance, rejection, and disapproval, and I release the destructible fire of God against them. I release God's revealed will, plans, purposes, and thoughts into the atmosphere and upon our marriage.

I prophesy my spouse and I are a perfect fit. We shall benefit, balance, and bring out the best in one another. We shall be suitable companions; equal to one another complimenting each other's character, stature, and persona.

In Jesus' name, I declare our marriage union is good and shall have a favorable reputation beginning now and all days to follow. Amen!

Day 23

In the same way, you wives, be submissive to your own husbands [subordinate, not as inferior, but out of respect for the responsibilities entrusted to husbands and their accountability to God, and so partnering with them] so that even if some do not obey the word [of God], they may be won over [to Christ] without discussion by the godly lives of their wives.
1 Peter 3:1
(Amplified Bible)

Prayer

Jesus, You are the way, the truth, and the life according to *John 14:6*. Shine Your light and bring clarity to those areas where the enemy has blinded my spouse or me, contributing to the strain of our marriage. Lord, I offer up every concern, frustration, and irreconcilable difference to You.

Release unto us godly obedience to respect each other at all times, regardless of whether we feel the other person deserves it. I ask that You do not allow unresolved offenses to become stumbling blocks in our marriage.

In Jesus' name, I bind spirits of harboring grudges, resentment, judgmentalism, and condemnation, and I release those spirits from their assignment to destroy the good in our marriage.

I declare God's Word and the Spirit of God is so strong in me that my spouse shall be won over to God by my godly demeanor, presence, and conduct. I declare the enemy is defeated, and the victory of God shall prevail in our marriage this day and forever.

I speak God's grace, mercy, peace, forgiveness, and goodwill over our marriage in Jesus' name. Amen!

Day 24

An excellent woman [one who is spiritual, capable, intelligent, and virtuous], who is he who can find her? Her value is more precious than jewels and her worth is far above rubies or pearls.

Proverbs 31:10
(Amplified Bible)

Prayer

You are a magnificent God, heavenly Father, because You see my true value and worth in our marriage.

I pray that You help my spouse and me see the value we each bring to our relationship. Use Your Holy Spirit to reveal those areas my spouse or I have failed to appreciate one another.

Right now, I come against spirits of superiority, gender discrimination, prejudice, and ungratefulness, and I render each of those spirits impotent and powerless. Whatever damage they have done to our marriage, I completely undo.

In Jesus' name, I release a spirit of unity, oneness, and harmony between my spouse and me. I declare we shall experience a greater level of connectedness. We shall vocalize our appreciation and acceptance of one another without apprehension and hesitation.

Now and forever, I speak God's progress and goodness over our marriage in Jesus' name. Amen!

Day 25

A virtuous and excellent wife [worthy of honor] is the crown of her husband, But she who shames him [with her foolishness] is like rottenness in his bones.
Proverbs 12:4
(Amplified Bible)

Prayer

Father in heaven, I praise You for Your holiness. You contain a spirit of excellence that cannot be matched.

As a spouse, I hope to be consistently virtuous, loving, and kind. Lord, I, ask that You shape and mold me to become like a crown to my spouse's head. I repent for any times I have shamed, disappointed, or offended my spouse. I repent for being rude, easily agitated, and hurting my spouse's feelings. Right now, I speak healing to those hurtful places, whether my spouse has brought it to my attention or not. Bring my spouse to a place of peace to accept my heartfelt apology.

I break agreement with every ill-tempered and impolite spirit. Let the words of my mouth be good medicine bringing healing, encouragement, and inspiration to my spouse. I shall no longer make a public spectacle of my spouse's weaknesses or flaws. I make a personal commitment to praise my spouse and hold my spouse in higher regard than I hold myself, because this is what pleases the Lord.

I speak God's healing, anointing, and reparation to every broken and fractured place, in Jesus' name, I pray. Amen!

Day 26

Better to live on a corner of the roof than share a house with a quarrelsome wife.
Proverbs 21:9
(New International Version)

Prayer

Dear Jesus, I worship You as the Prince of Peace. I pray for a reserved and tranquil spirit.

At this moment, I resist any critical or fault-finding spirit. In Jesus' name, I bind every combative, argumentative, and quarrelsome spirit and forbid them from operating in our marriage. I release God's peace and solidarity between my spouse and me. Make it possible for us to coexist with patience and understanding. Let us not be quick to snap to judgment or draw hasty conclusions. Instead, let us have a true listening ear when each are speaking.

May God's Word be the ultimate resource when making decisions and reaching agreements. Grant us a cooperative spirit when negotiating the things we are open to tolerate in our marriage, and the things we are unwilling to accept. Spread Your shalom peace upon us as a thick quilt on a cold, winter day. Permit the words that we speak to sweet as sugar and as peaceful as the morning sunrise.

I invoke God's covenant of peace, His unfailing mercies, and His unending kindness over our marriage this day and all days to follow, in Jesus' name. Amen!

Day 27

Some Pharisees came and tested him by asking, "Is it lawful for a man to divorce his wife?" "What did Moses command you?" he replied. They said, "Moses permitted a man to write a certificate of divorce and send her away." "It was because your hearts were hard that Moses wrote you this law," Jesus replied.
Mark 10:2-5
(New International Version)

Prayer

Heavenly Father, *Proverbs 2:6* says You give wisdom and from Your mouth comes knowledge and understanding. I praise You for the revelation knowledge unveiled regarding God's will for marriage. God never intended for couples to divorce. Instead, divorce was permitted as an alternative because of humanity's hardness of heart.

Right now, I smear the shed blood of Jesus over the hearts of my spouse and me. Help us to let go of any hardness of heart, unforgiveness, and bitterness in Jesus' name. Bind up all our wounds, both the ones we've shared and those we've kept secret and buried deep. I pray that we come into agreement with Your Word that divorce is not for us.

Let the blood of Jesus speak life over our marriage every time the enemy speaks death. Just as there are four layers to the earth: the crust, the mantle, the outer core, and inner core; I speak the blood of Jesus into the root, ground, every surface, and layer of our marriage. I decree our marriage will not die, but live according to *Psalm 118:17*.

The manifested glory of God shall be displayed over and over again, and prevail against all who oppose our marriage in Jesus' name. Amen!

Day 28

They sharpen their tongues like swords and aim cruel words like deadly arrows.
Psalm 64:3
(New International Version)

Prayer

Heavenly Father, I bless and magnify Your great name.

Help me to remember You have given a commandment to be kind and forgiving according to *Ephesians 4:32*. It is not a suggestion, but a heavenly requirement.

I pray You cure my spouse and me from a venomous tongue. Fumigate our lips and grant us the grace to abstain from all corrupt and profane speech. *Proverbs 18:21* states the tongue has the power of life and death. Empower us to speak words of life that nourish the spirit, body, and soul.

Right now, I repent for every obscene, hurtful, and inappropriate thing I have ever spoken to my spouse, and I nullify the power of those words. I detach myself from a vindictive spirit and remove any desire to want to get even and take matters into my own hands over perceived or actual wrongs. I apply the soothing, healing balm of Gilead to every offense. Grant us the capacity not to constantly recount and relive past grievances day in and day out.

I speak God's reformation, renewal, and restoration over our marriage, in Jesus' name. Amen!

Day 29

In the same way, you husbands must give honor to your wives. Treat your wife with understanding as you live together. She may be weaker than you are, but she is your equal partner in God's gift of new life. Treat her as you should so your prayers will not be hindered.

1 Peter 3:7
(New Living Translation)

Prayer

Heavenly Father, I thank You for my marriage. Thank You for revealing in Your Word how my spouse and I treat each other impacts the success of our prayers.

Our ability to treat each other fairly determines whether there is an open heaven or a closed heaven over us. So, I ask that You give us a willingness to follow Your blueprint for marriage.

Soften our hearts causing the both of us to dwell sympathetically with one another. Let there be an atmosphere of mutual submission and respect among us. Show us the proper way how to treat and love each other by the power of Your Holy Spirit.

Let us continually study the Word of God to show ourselves approved so our marriage can reflect what You had in mind when You put us together according to *2 Timothy 2:15*. Intensify our bond, closeness, connection, and intimacy so no one can come between us.

I declare we shall be best friends, God-fearing, faith-filled companions, effective communicators, collaborators, and faithful lovers in Jesus' name. Amen!

Day 30

Create in me a clean heart O, God. Renew a loyal spirit within me.

Psalms 51:10
(New Living Translation)

Prayer

Heavenly Father, You form the human spirit within a person (*Zechariah 12:1*). I give You thanks for Your ability to cleanse, refine, and transform my spouse and me.

Instill in us right attitudes, pure passions, motives, and ambitions. Lord, I invite You to take complete control and renovate our moral and mental nature, changing us from the inside out. Rebuild what needs to be rebuilt, and demolish what needs to be destroyed in Jesus' name.

Bring us both to a place of spiritual maturity where we willingly cast off the old and corrupt nature we once had. Breathe new life upon the areas of our marriage that needs a rebirth.

Let there be a cyclone release and a downpouring of the Holy Spirit working in us and through us. Provide us with supernatural inner strength to run this race of marriage with great endurance.

Bestow Your abundant blessings upon our marriage and cause it to shine like radiant jewels on a king's crown for the display of Your splendor in Jesus' mighty name. Amen!

Day 31

Blessed [anticipating God's presence, spiritually mature] are the pure in heart [those with integrity, moral courage, and good character], for they will see God.
Matthew 5:8
(Amplified Bible)

Prayer

Heavenly Father, I give You thanks because You keep my feet from stumbling and You make crooked paths straight for me.

With great humility, I say, "I am available to You." I pray my spouse and I are not wise in our own eyes. Instead, I ask for You to stir up our spirits to actively seek out Your presence so we can become vessels of respectable character.

In Jesus' name, I command all things that obstruct the move of the Holy Spirit in our marriage to be removed as far as the east is from the west. Gracious God, let Your government be established in our marriage from this moment forward.

2 Kings 1:10 says God sent fire from heaven on behalf of the prophet Elijah. I pray You send out Your flaming arrows to devour the enemy and decimate his camp on my behalf as well.

I command all crooked, lying, cocky, and irreverent spirits to bow down to the name of Jesus. Anything or any person intended to taint and spoil the good in our marriage, I command to scatter in seven directions in Jesus' name.

Sanctify us with the truth of Your word so we can possess the spiritual maturity You desire us to have in Jesus' name. Amen!

Day 32

Wives, be subject to your husbands [out of respect for their position as protector, and their accountability to God], as is proper and fitting in the Lord. Husbands, love your wives [with an affectionate, sympathetic, and selfless love that always seeks the best for them] and do not be embittered or resentful toward them [because of the responsibilities of marriage].
Colossians 3:18-19
(Amplified Bible)

Prayer

Heavenly Father, I invite You to counsel me with the skillfulness of Your eyes, hands, and heart to do the right thing for our marriage.

Merciful Father, I humble myself and ask Your forgiveness for the times my spouse or I withheld affection from one another. I repent for the times we did not respond to each other with patience, tenderness, and kindness You require. When we are tempted to turn our backs on one another because the responsibilities, pressure, and demands of marriage seem too much, cause our hearts to turn to each other rather than away from each other.

Right now, I forcefully resist all satanic barriers, strongholds, resistances, and rationalizations that keep my spouse and me from loving each other God's way. I place every adversarial force in a spiritual choke hold and render them bound and defeated.

I prophetically speak by faith no power of darkness shall be able to separate us in Jesus' name. Amen!

Day 33

But as the church is subject to Christ, so also wives ought to be subject to their husbands in everything [respecting both their position as protector and their responsibility to God as the head of the house]. Husbands, love your wives [seek the highest good for her and surround her with a caring, unselfish love], just as Christ also loved the church, and gave Himself up for her.

Ephesians 5:24-25
(Amplified Bible)

Prayer

Heavenly Father, I worship You as the God who works signs, wonders, and miracles.

You know best how our marriage should function since You are the One who designed it, outlined its' roles and responsibilities, and set the institution of marriage in motion.

Right now, I place our marriage in Your holy hands and ask that You rectify every wrong. Grant us the capacity to respect each other despite past failures, inadequacies, and imperfections. Endow us with the supernatural ability to seek the highest and greater good for one another and convict us when we don't.

In Jesus' name, I come against spirits of self-centeredness, self-absorbedness, and idolatry, and I paralyze them, strip them of their power, and render them completely inoperable. I decree these spirits shall no longer be present or a part of our marriage.

In Jesus' name, I speak God's complete goodness and wholeness to flood the very foundation of our marriage. Amen!

Day 34

For in this hope we were saved, but the hope that is seen is no hope at all. Who hopes for what he can already see?
Romans 8:24
(Berean Study Bible)

Prayer

Heavenly Father, You are my living hope.

I confess to moments of disbelief. I repent for having a little faith regarding the success of our marriage. During moments of hopelessness, remind me I am praying from a position of victory, rather than for victory. Jesus has already won the battle for me.

Today, I resist every spirit of despair and discouragement. I decree every momentary light affliction is leading my spouse and me to complete victory and is working for the advantage of our marriage. I exercise the power of my imagination and envision every origin of sorrow to flee from my heart. I lay every upsetting thing at the feet of Jesus, and leave it there, never to pick it up again.

I speak God's good success, victory, and happiness to the life of our marriage in Jesus' name. Amen!

Day 35

In the same way the Spirit [comes to us and] helps us in our weakness. We do not know what prayer to offer or how to offer it as we should but the Spirit Himself [know our need and at the right time] intercedes on our behalf with sighs and groanings too deep for words.

Romans 8:26
(Amplified Bible)

Prayer

Heavenly Father, I thank You for Your Holy Spirit. The Holy Spirit advocates and intercedes for the things I know not. Spirit of glory, counsel, and might fall fresh upon my spouse and me.

Merciful Father, I ask that Your Holy Spirit intercedes for our marriage morning, noon, and night.

Transform every weakness into strength, every failure into success, every vulnerability into security, and every deficiency into a strong point.

Lord, we need strength that comes from the power of Your Holy Spirit. Edify us, strengthen us, and build us up when we are completely exhausted, frustrated, and have no idea what to do. By the power of Your Holy Spirit, I decree counsel and sound judgment are ours, and we have insight and power according to *Proverbs 8:14*.

From this moment forward, I decree we possess the power to conquer challenges, power to overcome unexpected circumstances, power to persevere through testing and trouble, and power to overthrow every act of sabotage against our marriage.

Let a fresh wind of Your Holy Spirit blow upon us, disbursing every downcast spirit. Fill us to overflow of Your Holy Spirit and cause all things to become new and blessed in Jesus' name. Amen!

Day 36

Again, if two lie down together, then they keep warm; but how can one be warm alone? And though one can overpower him who is alone, two can resist him. A cord of three strands is not quickly broken.
Ecclesiastes 4:11-12
(Amplified Bible)

Prayer

Heavenly Father, thank You for revealing in Your Word that my spouse and I are stronger together than apart.

I lay our relationship before Your altar and ask that You bring us to a deeper place of oneness, unity, harmony, and togetherness. Grant each of us a willing spirit to pull together and work side by side to accomplish tasks in life.

Lord, grant us a more affectionate, loving, and caring spirit toward one another. Lead us on the path to build emotional, physical, and spiritual intimacy with one another satisfying each other in greater measures.

Under Christ's authority, I confront egotistical and conceited spirits, and command them to leave our marriage. In Jesus' name, I resist and disconnect my spouse and me from any spirit of isolation, and from any spirit of always having to be right.

I invite You, heavenly Father, to be the third cord to hold, bind, and connect us together until death do us part in Jesus' name. Amen!

Day 37

Both of them were righteous in the sight of God, observing all the Lord's commands and decrees blamelessly.

Luke 1:6
(New International Version)

Prayer

I thank You, heavenly Father, that You never take Your eyes off the righteous. Everything my spouse and I do is before You.

Compassionate God, I ask for You to grant my spouse and me an extraordinary ability to have integrity of heart. Let us be well-grounded, firm in faith, maintain genuine love for God, and love for one other. May we possess a spiritual discipline keeping Your laws inwardly and outwardly to the very end.

In Jesus' name, I come against all spirits of false pretense, crookedness, and insincerity, and I forbid them from influencing my spouse or me in any way, shape, or form. I declare the mind of Christ is in us to love each other well.

Today, I prophesy we shall honor, esteem, support, encourage, nurture, and meet the needs of each other with a willing, courteous, and gracious spirit in Jesus' name. Amen!

Day 38

I, the LORD, watch over it; I water it continually. I guard it day and night so that no one may harm it.

Isaiah 27:3
(New International Version)

Prayer

Heavenly Father, I'm thankful You neither sleep nor slumber. You are my shield, and Your protection is continuous.

I pray You guard our marriage from strange men and women whose motives are to tear down and destroy what You declare is holy. I cut the hand off of every hunter, and I decree the enemy cannot touch our marriage. Every spiritual arrow aimed at our marital relationship will miss and come to nothing in accordance with *Psalm 58:7.*

Lord, I invite You to be a bodyguard all around our marriage every second, minute, hour, month, and year. Water the dry spots in our marriage so it can grow, flourish, and thrive, becoming more alive and satisfying. May the Holy Spirit safeguard our marriage even while I am asleep, protecting our marriage from all hidden dangers, traps, and threats.

I release the voice of God against every antagonistic force speaking against our marriage. Strike the enemy with fear, cause him to cower down before You, and flee from our marriage. In every place where the enemy attempts to gain access to our marriage, let him be met with Your presence, because You are guarding it.

Thank you, God, that our marriage is under Your constant and consistent care. I receive the peace of God into my heart. Amen!

Day 39

A Song of Ascents. Blessed [happy and sheltered by God's favor] is everyone who fears the LORD [and worships Him with obedience], Who walks in His ways and lives according to His commandments. For you shall eat the fruit of [the labor of] your hands, You will be happy and blessed and it will be well with you. Your wife shall be like a fruitful vine within the innermost part of your house; Your children will be like olive plants around your table.

Psalm 128:1-3
(Amplified Bible)

Prayer

Dear Jesus, You are my inheritance and my exceedingly great reward. You are my High Priest who has established a better covenant with better promises for me according to *Hebrews 8:6*. Today, I position myself to receive every blessing You have secured for me.

Right now, I call the things that are not as though they are, and I declare it is well with my spouse and me (*Isaiah 3:10*). Our marriage will endure good and unpleasant times, storms and sunshine, trials and peaceful moments, and struggles and triumphs.

I come into agreement with God's word, and call our marriage and home immensely blessed. I decree we shall be blessed with the blessings of heaven above and the blessings that lie deep. We shall be fruitful, prosperous, increase abundantly, abound in wisdom, and enjoy divine sufficiency in all things in Jesus' name. Amen!

Day 40

And now, my daughter, don't be afraid. I will do for you all you ask. All the people of my town know that you are a woman of noble character.

Ruth 3:11
(New International Version)

Prayer

Heavenly Father, You are reliable, dependable, and faithful. I confess with my mouth that I know You can do all things and no purpose of Yours can thwarted (*Job 42:2*).

Today, I pray my life and the life of my spouse will exemplify a living, testament of God's workmanship. Change what needs to be changed about us, and grant us a willing spirit to make the necessary adjustments to enhance our marriage. Give us a new name and an improved identity in any area where our reputation has been muddied and defamed.

I decree people around us shall be left stunned and speechless as they witness our spiritual metamorphosis and transformation. Having noble character shall be as common for us as a lawyer who wears a suit.

I speak God's goodness, greatness, and glorification over our marriage today and always in Jesus' name. Amen!

Day 41

Now write another decree in the king's name in behalf of the Jews as seem best to you, and seal it with the king's signet ring-for no document written in the king's name and sealed with his ring can be revoked.

Esther 8:8
(New International Version)

Prayer

I am grateful heavenly Father, for the power Your Word carries. *Matthew 24:35* says heaven and earth shall pass away but Your Word shall never pass away. I rejoice today because no one can fight against You and win.

Today, I ask that You write a new decree in the heavens for our marriage, one of blessings, favor, and honor that forbids the enemy from stealing, killing, or destroying it. I implore You to seal this decree with Jesus' shed blood so that no entity, person, act of witchcraft, sorcery, evil incantation, or demonic divination can overturn it. Seize all those who object to our marriage with a godly sorrow and lead them to true repentance before You.

Mighty God, speak a blessing over our marriage which cannot be revoked in Jesus' name. Amen!

Day 42

There is no divination against Jacob, no evil omens against Israel. It will now be said of Jacob and of Israel, "See what God has done!"

Numbers 23:23
(New International Version)

Prayer

Heavenly Father, You are a curse breaker.

I apply the blood of the Lamb upon our marriage, and declare it is free from every source of divination, evil omen, magic, spell, witchcraft, evil prayer, and sorcery, past, present, and future.

You have appointed me over nations and kingdoms to uproot and to tear down, to destroy, and to overthrow, and to build and to plant according to *Jeremiah 1:10*. I uproot every demonic entity and overthrow the plans of wickedness orchestrated against our marriage in the matchless name of Jesus. I declare no weapons or schemes fashioned anywhere against our marital relationship shall prosper.

Lord, I ask that You perplex the wicked, and confound their tongue and words. Under Christ's anointing, I decree every evil thought, intention, and practice directed at our marriage will fail miserably. What the enemy meant for evil, God will turn it around for our marriage's benefit.

All who behold our marriage, shall say, "Look what God has done!" All will marvel at how You destroyed and completely annihilated evil, wicked, lying, and deceitful men's plots.

I praise You in advance as You display Your power that man might believe that the Holy One of Israel is truly the defender of our house and marriage in Jesus' name. Amen!

Day 43

But God said to Balaam, "Do not go with them. You must not put a curse on those people, because they are blessed."
Numbers 22:12
(New International Version)

Prayer

Heavenly Father, You are a fortified tower for me. I can run to You in faith, and I experience safety and security in boundless ways.

I thank You Lord for every blessing You have spoken over our marriage. Your benediction of blessing is so great and powerful that it nullifies the evil wishes of every witch, warlock, medium, sorcerer, or enemy known and unknown.

I invoke the power of *Numbers 22:12*, and declare no man can curse our marriage because God has ordained it and blessed it. In Jesus' name, I cancel every word curse and ill-intended prayer spoken out against me, my spouse, or our marriage. I decree we shall not eat the bread of wickedness. Instead, we shall partake the cup of the Lord's blessing every day of our marriage.

With the Lord's hammer, I break every evil altar erected in our marriage, and I erect the altar of the Lord. Light of God burst through, shine bright, and cause Your blessings to flood and overtake our marriage in Jesus' name. Amen!

Day 44

Like a fluttering sparrow or a darting swallow, an underserved curse will not land on its intended victim.

Proverbs 26:2
(New Living Translation)

Prayer

Heavenly Father, You are a liberator of curses. You specialize in setting captives free. *Proverbs 26:2* confirms no curse can come against a person who has done nothing to deserve it.

Today, I ask that You cultivate all fallow ground in our marriage, making it productive again. *Galatians 3:13* confirms that I am redeemed from the curse of the law because Jesus became a curse for me. So, in Jesus' name, I break every word, generational, and ancestral curse through the blood of Jesus and through the finish work of the cross that would give the enemy a legal right to afflict our marriage with troubles, misfortunes, and hardships. I cancel any agreement my spouse or I ignorantly entered into with the enemy due to a lack of knowledge of God's Word.

I declare no curse shall come and touch our marriage for the blood of Jesus speaks for us, pardons us, delivers us, saves us, protects us, and preserves us.

Our marriage shall remain divinely protected, blessed, favored in Jesus' name. Amen!

Day 45

When the Syrians attacked, Elisha prayed, "O LORD, strike these men blind!" The Lord answered his prayer and struck them blind.

2 Kings 6:18
(Good News Translation)

Prayer

God, You are my fortress and high tower. I praise You for being my defender and my help in my hour of need.

I ask that You arise, merciful Father, with Your weapons of war and execute vengeance upon the enemy of our marriage in Jesus' name. I, ask Lord, that You strike the enemy, every principality, power, ruler of darkness, and spiritual wickedness in high places with blindness so the eyes of the enemy cannot wreck our marriage. Smite every evil adversary of our marriage with Your fist and fury. Weary the heart of the adversary who would like to see our marriage fail and protect us Lord from the evil one.

I thank You, God, that I can lean on and trust You to deliver our marriage from every devilish attack. Now, I decree our marriage is unseeable to the eyes of the enemy.

I speak total healing and deliverance over our marriage from every malicious attack and assault in Jesus' incomparable name. Amen!

Day 46

This is what the LORD says: "As when juice is still found in a cluster of grapes and people say, 'Don't destroy it, there is still a blessing in it,' so will I do in behalf of my servants; I will not destroy them all."
Isaiah 65:8
(New International Version)

Prayer

Heavenly Father You are my support system. You don't cast me away and forget about me. I thank You for Your faithfulness.

I ask that You remain an impenetrable shield and a gigantic fire wall all around our marriage.

Many spectators say, our marriage is no good, there is no reason to preserve it, and even think I am crazy for staying. However, I confess that I walk by faith and not by sight. I trust in the providential care of the Lord. I confess with my mouth I am observing our marriage with spiritual lenses, and declare there is still a blessing in it.

At this very moment, I put every sin, iniquity, and transgression under the shed blood of Jesus for complete pardoning. I speak a supernatural and inexplicable reversal of everything negative, deficient, and abominable in our marriage.

I declare I am God's child and I ask, Lord, that You speak a word over our marriage now, which says, "I will not destroy it," according to *Isaiah 65:8*.

I appreciate the success You hold in store for our relationship, and I receive all of Your blessings of protection, preservation, safety, and stability for our marriage. Amen!

Day 47

In our life in the Lord, however, woman is not independent of man, nor is man of woman. For as woman was made from man, in the same way man is born of woman, and it is God who brings everything into existence.

1 Corinthians 11:11-12
(Good News Translation)

Prayer

Heavenly Father, I'm thankful You joined us together and regard us as equals. I'm grateful You have made it plain we are not superior to the other.

Help my spouse and me to realize we are not each other's enemy even during difficult times.

In the power of Jesus' name, I come against every spirit of separatism, exclusivism, and superiority. I command every controlling, overbearing, and domineering spirit to bow to the name of Jesus.

I speak God's healing, wholeness, and good emotional well-being over us. I pronounce the name of Jesus over every weak area, and declare God's reparations to overtake every shaky and unsteady foundation in our marriage.

I prophetically speak by faith, our marriage is becoming stronger by the day, and my spouse and I are merging as one in Christ in the wonderful name of Jesus. Amen!

Day 48

But I want you to understand that Christ is the head (authority over) of every man, and man is the head of woman, and God is the head of Christ.

1 Corinthians 11:3
(Amplified Bible)

Prayer

Heavenly Father, You are the chief cornerstone of our marriage. I give You full access and authority to rule and reign in our marriage.

Cause those things that are out of Your divine order to come back into Your alignment. Transform our marriage into a new and improved version of what we currently have. Let it represent a union of mutual respect, comforts, and blessings.

I declare Christ is head over the husband, and the husband is the head over the wife. I'm grateful submission does not mean insubordination or inferiority, but rather a recognition of rank. Just as Jesus Christ was subordinate to the Father, but also equal and one with the Father, so should a husband-and-wife ought to be.

So, Lord, make us one. Let us be of one mind, one faith, and one spirit. Let our marriage reflect Christ's love for the church.

Right now, I cast down every foolish idea and doctrine that exalts itself against the knowledge of God, and I capture every misinterpretation of the Bible regarding husband and wife's marital relationship and bring it into the obedience of Jesus Christ.

In the same way that the head cannot operate without the body, so a husband-and-wife ought to not seek to be separate from one another. Let God be true and every man a liar in accordance with *Romans 3:4*. Amen!

Day 49

No one should seek their own good, but the good of others.
1 Corinthians 10:24
(New International Version)

Prayer

Heavenly Father, You are a selfless God. You loved my spouse and me even when we were enemies of God (*Romans 5:10*). Thank You Lord for the example You have modeled and set regarding true, genuine love.

Love is patient, kind, not envious, not boastful, not proud, not selfish, not easily angered, doesn't keep record of wrongs, and delights in the truth (*1 Corinthians 13:4-6*).

I repent for any moments I operated in a spirit of selfishness and brought conflict, confusion, or chaos to our marriage. I ask that You give my spouse and me a new heart; a selfless heart to love one another affectionately, tenderly, and holding each other in greater esteem than we hold ourselves.

Help us to remember to build each other up: to encourage, support, inspire, defend, and protect at all times, not necessarily by emotion, but rather by conviction to God and marital covenant.

I speak Your immeasurable blessings upon our marriage; blessings that cannot be counted, fathomed, or imagined by the human mind in Jesus' name. Amen!

Day 50

Though the mountains be shaken and the hills be removed, yet my unfailing love for you will not be shaken nor my covenant of peace be removed," says the LORD, who has compassion on you.

Isaiah 54:10
(New International Version)

Prayer

Heavenly Father, You are the God over the hills and the valley. You are God over every challenge and dilemma in our marriage.

Right now, I yield to Your presence and ask that You fill my heart, mind, home, and marriage with Your comforting peace.

In Jesus' name, I bind spirits of bickering, strife, power struggles, and petty quarrels, and I release the fire of God against them. I speak a cease fire to every argumentative, accusatory, and assaulting spirit. I lay a spiritual ax to the root of every source of friction in our marriage. I decree there shall be no more tug-a wars, rivalry, and unhealthy competitions between us.

I ask for You to deploy twelve legions of angels to enforce Your covenant of peace in our marriage in accordance with *Matthew 26:53*. I activate the power of *Isaiah 54:10*, and call forth Your safety, happiness, health, prosperity, and serenity for our marriage.

I decree this covenant of peace shall not be changed by things above, in, or below the earth, in Jesus' name. Amen.

Day 51

There is no fear in love [dread does not exist]. But perfect (complete, full-grown) love drives out fear, because fear involves [the expectation of divine] punishment, so the one who is afraid [of God's judgment] is not perfected in love [has not grown into sufficient understanding of God's love].

1 John 4:18
(Amplified Bible)

Prayer

Your grace, heavenly Father, is sufficient for me. I am grateful for the love You poured out for me through Your son, Jesus. Thank You for reminding me that true love has no element of fear in it.

Equip my spouse and I to love each other in a healthy kind of way. Let personal insecurities melt away like wax, and let Your confidence arise speedily within us.

In Jesus' name, I detach my spouse and me from every anxious and unhealthy jealous spirit. I come against all tormenting and fearful spirits causing emotional and mental disturbances, and I command those spirits to depart now in the powerful name of Jesus.

God, release Your whirlwind against every evil entity conspiring to ruin and break up our marriage. I ask that You scatter and paralyze the enemy by Your incomparable power. Immobilize all of the enemy's operations and make every adversary of our marriage suddenly afraid. *Mark 10:9* says what God has joined together let no man separate, and I petition the court of heaven for a release of Your strongest angels to enforce this marital promise.

I decree the scepter of the wicked shall not rest upon our marriage according to *Psalms 125:2*. My spouse and I shall not be burnt out, worn out, or grow tired of each other.

I prophesy our marriage shall persevere in Jesus' name. Amen!

Day 52

No one has ever seen God at any time. But if we love one another [with unselfish concern], God abides in us, and His love [the love that is His essence abides in us and] is completed and perfected in us.
1 John 4:12
(Amplified Bible)

Prayer

Heavenly Father, I thank You that Your love towards me is perfected and it is bullet-proof. Thank You for revealing in Your word that humanity's love towards God is brought to maturity by the exercise of love towards our brethren, including one's spouse.

I repent now for the times I have not loved my spouse well. In Jesus' name, I ask that You bless my spouse and me with a perfect union that excludes all self-interest.

Let us never forget that the true nature of love is not self-serving, but self-sacrificing. Forgive the both of us for the times we were impatient, unkind, envious, boastful, proud, easily angered, and kept record of wrongs. Give us a new heart that reflects the essence of Christ, and seeks the greater good for one another.

Replace the bad memories housed in our minds with new and positive reflections that keep us optimistic about our future together in Jesus' name.

I speak God's reconciliation, restoration, and reparation over our marriage. Amen!

Day 53

When you make a vow to God, do not delay to fulfill it. He has no pleasure in fools; fulfill your vow. It is better not to make a vow than to make one and not fulfill it.

Ecclesiastes 5:4-5
(New International Version)

Prayer

I thank You, God, that You are a spirit. You are not like man and cannot lie (*Numbers 23:19*). Every Word spoken from Your lips is producing life for our marriage.

Help us to remember marriage requires commitment, not only to each other but to You. When we spoke our marital vows, You were present, listening, and sealed the covenant. Our marriage is ordained, sanctified, and blessed by Your lips and hands.

Grant us the spiritual wisdom to know no one can break a vow to God without it becoming sin. Help us Lord to demonstrate the spiritual maturity that is required to keep our marital vows. Let us not be led by our emotions, but rather by Your spirit.

I forcefully resist every irresponsible and immature spirit, and I release a spirit of accountability and maturity upon my spouse and me. Transform us into people who keep their word and honor their commitments in Jesus' name. Amen!

Day 54

"Is it not my family God has chosen? Yes, he has made an everlasting covenant with me. His agreement is arranged and guaranteed in every detail. He will ensure my safety and success."

2 Samuel 23:5
(New Living Translation)

Prayer

Heavenly Father, You alone are the keeper of my house. You maintain my lot and make it secure (*Psalm 16:15*).

I cordially invite You to properly order all things in our marriage. I thank You that no personal failures or mistakes can undo Your desire and promise to bless our marriage.

Today, I decree our marriage shall remain in the hands of God. Every covenant promise of safety and success for marriage is ours. Therefore, I rejoice, and my heart is flooded with gladness.

Our marriage is marred with the blood of Jesus Christ, who speaks good things on our behalf. Jesus, I thank You for caring about the fate of our marriage. I give You praise that our marriage is divinely protected by You forever and always in Jesus' name.

May Your blessings always supersede the doubters and opinions of man. Our marriage shall remain blessed, prospered, and favored at all times, and in every season in Jesus' name. Amen!

Day 55

In the days of His earthly life, Jesus offered up both [specific] petitions and [urgent] supplications [for that which He needed] with fervent crying and tears to the One who was [always] able to save Him from death, and He was heard because of His reverent submission toward God [His sinlessness and His unfailing determination to do the Father's will].

Hebrews 5:7
(Amplified Bible)

Prayer

Heavenly Father, You are my Redeemer. You have delivered my life from the snare of death.

Through Jesus Christ, the covenant of death has been completely annulled. Therefore, I choose to believe Your death and resurrection has redeemed our marriage from every spirit of death as well.

I give You praise that every tear I've shed is before Your throne, counted, and has never escaped Your eyes. You give me beauty for ashes, oil of joy for mourning, and a garment of praise for any spirit of heaviness (*Isaiah 61:3*).

In Jesus' name, I forcefully oppose all spirits of depression, oppression, and suicide, and I command those spirits to submit to the authority of Jesus Christ.

I silence every voice speaking death over our marriage, and decree resurrection life is taking over every lifeless place in our relationship for the glory of God. In Jesus' name, I break all death cycles and decree our marriage shall live, flourish, and persevere.

From this day forward, may my spouse and me experience life and life more abundantly in our marriage in Jesus' name. Amen!

Day 56

For I will turn toward you [with favor and regard] and make you fruitful and multiply you, and I will establish and confirm My covenant with you.

Leviticus 26:9
(Amplified Bible)

Prayer

I thank You heavenly Father, for Your devotion to establish and confirm Your covenant to bless my spouse and me.

I ask that You turn Your face with favor and regard to our marriage immediately. I decree now there shall be no financial lack or limitations in our marriage. We shall rise out of every impoverished condition.

Proverbs 3:33 confirms You bless the home of the righteous. In every place where the enemy has robbed us of our marital assets, I decree a sevenfold return of everything the enemy has stolen in accordance with *Proverbs 6:31*.

I speak God's abundance, prosperity, wealth, and inexplicable increase over our marital finances in Jesus' name. Amen!

Day 57

A Psalm of David. The LORD is my Shepherd [to feed, to guide and to shield me], I shall not want.

Psalms 23:1
(Amplified Bible)

Prayer

You are a good Shepherd, heavenly Father. In You I have sufficiency in all things.

Right now, I exercise my authority in Christ, and I rebuke and cast out every spirit of lack, stagnation, reoccurring setbacks, and bankruptcy. I declare the prosperity and advancement of the Lord over our marital property, employment, credit, investments, and ministries.

Today, I ask You to grant my spouse and me spiritual revelation regarding what employment opportunities to accept, and which ones to walk away from. Lord, order our steps. Close those doors and opportunities that are not fruitful for us, and lay plainly before us the path You want us to take.

Pave pathways for us that make us economically and financially strong for the benefit of our marriage, and the advancement of Your heavenly kingdom, this day and forever. Amen!

Day 58

For you are God, O Sovereign LORD. Your words are truth, and you have promised these good things to your servant. And now, may it please you to bless the house of your servant, so that it may continue forever before you. For you have spoken, and when you grant a blessing to your servant, O Sovereign LORD, it is an eternal blessing.

2 Samuel 7:28-29
(New Living Translation)

Prayer

I thank You heavenly Father, that You are a God of abundance. When You bless, You bless eternally.

So, I ask that You bless my spouse and me with godly wisdom, knowledge, strength, good health, prosperity, advancements, promotions, peace of mind, and happiness. Let Your increase be so great upon our marriage and financial assets, that there is a never-ending residue that flows onto all future generations to follow in Jesus' name.

I decree now that failure and defeat shall not be affiliated with our names, marital assets, or legacy. I prophesy now that we are going from faith to faith, strength to strength, and glory to ever-increasing glory this day and forever.

I thank You for this eternal blessing that our marriage shall remain supernaturally blessed throughout all time, and for all generations to come, in Jesus' name. Amen!

Day 59

Praise the LORD. Blessed are those who fear the LORD, who find great delight in his commands. Their children will be mighty in the land; the generation of the upright will be blessed. Wealth and riches are in their houses, and their righteousness endures forever.

Psalm 112:1-3
(New International Version)

Prayer

Heavenly Father, You are El Shaddai, the God of more than enough. Whenever You bless and meet a need, there is no scarcity.

I confess with my mouth that I respect You and delight in Your Word. Now, I decree any children my spouse or me conceive together shall be mighty in the land and do good works.

I cancel every word curse spoken over the life and body of our children and all future descendants. I nullify the power of every word curse, and decree God who began a good work in our offspring shall bring it to completion until the day of Jesus Christ (*Philippians 1:6*).

I decree wealth and riches are in our home, and that the divine favor of God rests upon our finances. The blessings of the Lord actively pursue and overtake us. We increase exceedingly because the spirit of the Lord rests upon us endowing us with an extraordinary ability to accumulate wealth from all financial pursuits, and from hidden riches in secret places.

Our marriage, home, and finances shall reflect God's kingdom where there is no lack. Thank You, Jesus, for allowing our marriage to remain blessed, prosperous, and favored at all times, and in every season, in Jesus' name. Amen!

Day 60

When Jesus had received the sour wine, He said, "It is finished." And He bowed His head and [voluntarily] gave up His spirit.
John 19:30
(Amplified Bible)

Prayer

I praise You, heavenly Father, because You do all things well. You never leave anything incomplete or undone. Through the birth, death, and resurrection of Your son, Jesus, every benefit and blessing of the blood covenant is accessible to me. Here and now, I claim it for my life and marriage.

Jesus was the perfect atonement for every sin, iniquity, transgression, and debt that my spouse or I owed. I declare that the enemy's plans to assassinate our marriage have been completely obliterated by the finished work of the cross. Jesus Christ of Nazareth has secured victory for us.

I lift and elevate the Lord's altar, and I proudly pronounce God's joy, happiness, peace, healing, restoration, deliverance, prosperity, and salvation over us.

The infallible Word of God shall be fulfilled in our marriage, and all the adversarial forces of hell will be powerless to stop it in the almighty name of Jesus.

By Your dunamis power, I speak life and total victory over our marriage today and forever. Amen!

Married Couples And Their Years Together!

Jonathan and Skye Padilla

Bridge Church, Murrieta, CA

Married eleven years!

Harrison and Mary Makau

Married thirty-three years!

Founders of Transforming Life
International Ministry

Aaron and Rosie Belton

Married thirty-two years!

Jan and Oz

Married fifty-one years!

Bridge Church, Murrieta, CA

Richard and Jan Lauletta

Married fifty-eight years!

God's Grace Healing Room, Temecula, CA

Robert and Patricia "Diahann" Johnson

Married thirty years!

Founders of Christian Resting Place Ministries

Chris and Ivy Jones

Married twenty-seven years!

Bridge Church, Murrieta, CA

J.T. and Earline Burnside

Nykia Coleman's paternal grandparents

Married over fifty years!

Pastors Corey and Amber White

Married thirteen years!

Avery and Nykia Coleman

Married twenty-four years!

About The Author

Nykia Coleman is a minister, prayer warrior, author, and conference speaker. Nykia had her first, personal encounter with God when she was nine years old, while interceding on her mother's behalf. Since then, Nykia has made praying for others her life's work.

Nykia holds a master's degree in Education and a bachelor's degree in Sociology. Nykia also completed the Billy Graham's School of Evangelism Training, as well as, the Billy Graham's ReIgnite Training, and is excited about winning souls for Jesus Christ. Moreover, she has completed training through the School of Prayer on the

Art of Intercession. Nykia is known throughout her family, neighbors, community, and church as a woman of prayer. Nykia frequently utilizes the skills acquired from previous healing room training, and instruction from the Benny Hinn Institute when praying for the sick.

Nykia has been married to her husband, Avery Michael Coleman, for over twenty years. Together, they share three beautiful children.

Recently, Nykia launched her own prayer ministry, Pray4Breakthrough, where people can submit prayer requests for their specific needs. Nykia firmly believes God's house shall be a house of prayer in accordance with Mark 11:17.

To write the author:

Attention: Nykia Coleman

30724 Benton Road Ste C-302 #378

Winchester, CA 92596

Email: pray4breakthrough@yahoo.com

To find out more about Nykia or to donate to her prayer ministry, you can visit online:

Website: www.pray4breakthrough.com

Other Books By Nykia Coleman

PRAY-4-BREAKTHROUGH LESS THAN 5 MINUTE PRAYERS TO SPEAK OVER YOUR CHILDREN

ORAR POR AVANCE ORACIONES DE MENOS DE 5 MINUTOS PARA HABLAR SOBRE SUS HIJOS